P9-EFI-553

Hachiko

The True Story of a Loyal Dog

written by PAMELA S. TURNER

illustrated by YAN NASCIMBENE

Houghton Mifflin Company
Boston 2004

www.houghtonmifflinbooks.com

The text of this book is set in 11-point Christina.
The illustrations are watercolor, reproduced in full color.

Library of Congress Cataloging-in-Publication Data

Turner, Pamela S.
Hachiko / by Pamela S. Turner ; illustrated by Yan Nascimbene.
        p. cm.
Summary: Relates the true story of a dog who accompanied his master to and from a Tokyo train station for a year and, after his master died, continued to wait for him there every day for many years.
ISBN 0-618-14094-8 (hardcover)
1. Hachiko (Dog). 2. Dogs—Japan—Tokyo—Biography. [1. Hachiko (Dog). 2. Dogs.] I. Nascimbene, Yan, ill. II. Title.
  SF426.5.T87 2004
  636.7′00952—dc21
                                    2002155546

Manufactured in the United States of America
WOZ 10 9 8 7 6 5 4 3 2 1

For Travis, Kelsey, and Connor

—P. S.T.

To Simca and Cicciolina.
And to Mark, with many thanks for the workspace.

—Y.N.

There is a statue of my old friend at the entrance to Shibuya Station. His bronze feet are bright and shiny, polished by thousands of friendly hands. There is a sign that says, simply, "Loyal dog Hachiko." I close my eyes and remember the day we met, so long ago.

When I was six years old, my family moved to a little house in Tokyo near the Shibuya train station. At first the trains frightened me. But after a while, I grew to enjoy their power and the furious noises they made. One day I begged Mama to take me to meet Papa as he came home on the afternoon train. She laughed and said, "Kentaro, you have become big and brave, just like a samurai!" Together we walked to the station.

It was spring, and the day was clear and cold. There were tiny carts all around the station, selling snacks, newspapers, and hundreds of other things to the crowds of people rushing by. Ladies in kimonos walked carefully, trying to keep their white *tabi* socks away from the grime of the streets. Businessmen strode about, hurrying home or to catch another train. Mama and I had stopped near the station entrance when I noticed the dog.

He was sitting quietly, all alone, by a newspaper stand. He had thick, cream-colored fur, small pointed ears, and a broad, bushy tail that curved up over his back. I wondered if the dog was a stray, but he was wearing a nice leather harness and looked healthy and strong.

His brown eyes were fixed on the station entrance.

Just then, Papa appeared. He was chatting with an older man. The dog bounded over to the man, his entire body wiggling and quivering with delight. His eyes shone, and his mouth curled up into something that looked, to me, just like a smile.

"Ah, Kentaro! You see, Dr. Ueno, you are not the only one who has someone to welcome him," said Papa. He introduced us to the older man. "Dr. Ueno works with me at Tokyo Imperial University."

"What is your dog's name?" I asked timidly. The dog was beautiful, but his sharp face reminded me of a wolf's. I grabbed Mama's kimono and stepped behind her, just in case.

"Don't be afraid," said Dr. Ueno kindly. "This is Hachiko. He is big, but still a puppy. He walks me to the station every morning and waits for me to come home every afternoon. I think Hachiko stores up all his joy, all day long, and then lets it out all at once!"

Hachiko stood wagging his tail next to Dr. Ueno. I reached out to touch him, and he bounced forward and sniffed my face. I yelped and jumped back behind Mama.

They all laughed. "Oh, Kentaro, don't worry—he just wants to get to know you," said Dr. Ueno. "Dogs can tell a lot about people just by smelling them. Why, Hachiko probably knows what you ate for lunch!"

I sniffed my hand, but it didn't smell like rice balls to me. I reached out and touched Hachiko gently on the shoulder. "His fur is so thick and soft," I said. "Like a bear's."

"Dogs like Hachiko once hunted bears in the north, where it is very cold and snowy," said Dr. Ueno, kneeling down next to me and rubbing Hachiko's ears.

From that day on, I went to the station almost every afternoon. But I no longer went to see the trains. I went to see Hachiko. He was always there, waiting near the newspaper stand. I often saved a morsel from my lunch and hid it in one of my pockets. Hachiko would sniff me all over, wagging his tail, until he found a sticky bit of fish or soybean cake. Then he would nudge me with his nose, as if to say, "Give me my prize!" When it was cold, I would bury my face in the thick ruff of creamy fur around his neck.

One day in May, I was waiting at the station with Hachiko. The moment I saw Papa, I knew something was wrong. He was alone, and he walked hunched over, staring sadly at the gray pavement under his feet.

"What's the matter, Papa?" I asked him anxiously, standing with one hand on Hachiko's broad head. He sighed. "Kentaro, let's go home." Hachiko's bright brown eyes followed us as we walked away, but he stayed behind, waiting for Dr. Ueno.

When we got home, Papa told us that Dr. Ueno had died that morning at the university. I was stunned. "But what will happen to Hachiko?" I asked, blinking hard to keep the tears back. "What will he do?"

"I don't know," said Papa. "Perhaps Dr. Ueno's relatives will take him in."

"What about tonight?" I asked. "Can we go see if he is all right?"

Papa was very sad and tired, but he walked with me back to Shibuya Station. Hachiko was curled up by the newspaper stand. He wagged his tail when he saw us. Papa and I gave him water in an old chipped bowl and some food. Hachiko ate and drank, but he kept looking up toward the station entrance for Dr. Ueno. Papa and I left even sadder than we had come.

The next day, I went back to check on Hachiko, but he was not there. Papa told me that Hachiko had been taken several miles away to live with some of Dr. Ueno's relatives. "But I'll never see him again!" I cried. "Why can't he live with us?"

"We don't have room for a dog," protested Papa. "And Hachiko really belongs to Dr. Ueno's relatives, now that Dr. Ueno is dead. Hachiko is better off having a home than sitting at a train station."

But Hachiko had other ideas. A few days later he was back at Shibuya Station, patiently waiting, his brown eyes fixed on the entrance. Hachiko had run back to his old home, and from there to Shibuya Station.

Mama and Papa let me take food and water to Hachiko every day. Mama grumbled a bit about the food, saying we couldn't afford to feed a big bear like Hachiko, but she always seemed to cook more rice than we could eat.

Other people at the station took an interest in Hachiko. Men and women who rode Papa and Dr. Ueno's train stopped by to scratch his ears and say a few kind words. One day I saw an old man filling Hachiko's water bowl as Hachiko licked his hand. The old man's hair was streaked with gray, and he was stooped, as if he had spent most of his life bent over the ground. But his eyes were as sharp and bright as Hachiko's.

"Are you young Kentaro?" the old man asked. I nodded. "I'm Mr. Kobayashi. I was Dr. Ueno's gardener.

"Dr. Ueno told me that you and Hachiko often wait for the afternoon train together."

"Do you still take care of the house where Dr. Ueno lived?" I asked.

"Yes," said Mr. Kobayashi. "Hachiko comes back to the house every night to sleep on the porch. But in the morning, he walks to the station just like he did with Dr. Ueno. When the last train leaves the station, he returns home."

We were both silent. Then I asked, "Do you think Hachiko knows that Dr. Ueno died?"

Mr. Kobayashi said thoughtfully, "I don't know, Kentaro. Perhaps he still hopes that Dr. Ueno will return someday. Or perhaps he knows Dr. Ueno is dead, but he waits at the station to honor his master's memory."

As the years passed and Hachiko got older, he became very stiff and could barely walk to Shibuya Station. But still he went, every day. People began collecting money to build a statue of Hachiko at the station. Papa, Mama, and I all gave money, and we were very happy when the statue was placed next to the spot Hachiko had waited for so many years.

One chilly morning I woke to the sound of Mama crying. "What's wrong?" I asked as I stumbled into the kitchen. Papa sat silently at the table, and Mama turned her tear-stained face to me. "Hachiko died last night at Shibuya Station," she choked. "Still waiting for Dr. Ueno."

I was seventeen, and too big to cry. But I went into the other room and did not come out for a long time.

Later that day we all went to the station. To our great surprise, Hachiko's spot near the newspaper stand was covered in flowers placed there by his many friends.

Old Mr. Kobayashi was there. He shuffled over to me and put a hand on my shoulder.

"Hachiko didn't come back to the house last night," he said quietly. "I walked to the station and found him. I think his spirit is with Dr. Ueno's, don't you?"

"Yes," I whispered.

The Story Behind the Story

Some years ago, my family moved to Tokyo, and we rented a home not far from Shibuya Station. Everyone, it seemed, knew that Hachiko's statue was the place to meet at the huge train station. No matter what time of day or night I visited Shibuya, I would always see someone standing near the large bronze dog, with eyes searching the crowd.

My Japanese friends told me Hachiko's story. Hachiko was born in northern Japan in November 1923, and a few months later he was sent to Dr. Ueno in Tokyo. When Dr. Ueno died on May 21, 1925, they had been together for just over a year.

In October 1932, a newspaper reporter wrote a story about Hachiko. The headline read: "A Faithful Dog Awaits the Return of Master Dead for Seven Years." People began traveling to Shibuya from all over Japan, just to pet loyal Hachiko.

Hachiko's vigil at Shibuya Station lasted almost ten years. He died March 7, 1935. One year earlier, a bronze statue of Hachiko had been placed near the entrance to Shibuya Station, right next to the spot where he always waited for Dr. Ueno. There is an old photo of the real Hachiko next to the bronze one, surrounded by a crowd of people. Hachiko seems to be wondering what all the fuss is about.

"Hachiko didn't come back to the house last night," he said quietly. "I walked to the station and found him. I think his spirit is with Dr. Ueno's, don't you?"

"Yes," I whispered.

The big bronze statue of Hachiko is a very famous meeting place. Shibuya Station is enormous now, and hundreds of thousands of people travel through it every day. People always say to each other, "Let's meet at Hachiko." Today Hachiko is a place where friends and family long separated come together again.

The Story Behind the Story

Some years ago, my family moved to Tokyo, and we rented a home not far from Shibuya Station. Everyone, it seemed, knew that Hachiko's statue was the place to meet at the huge train station. No matter what time of day or night I visited Shibuya, I would always see someone standing near the large bronze dog, with eyes searching the crowd.

My Japanese friends told me Hachiko's story. Hachiko was born in northern Japan in November 1923, and a few months later he was sent to Dr. Ueno in Tokyo. When Dr. Ueno died on May 21, 1925, they had been together for just over a year.

In October 1932, a newspaper reporter wrote a story about Hachiko. The headline read: "A Faithful Dog Awaits the Return of Master Dead for Seven Years." People began traveling to Shibuya from all over Japan, just to pet loyal Hachiko.

Hachiko's vigil at Shibuya Station lasted almost ten years. He died March 7, 1935. One year earlier, a bronze statue of Hachiko had been placed near the entrance to Shibuya Station, right next to the spot where he always waited for Dr. Ueno. There is an old photo of the real Hachiko next to the bronze one, surrounded by a crowd of people. Hachiko seems to be wondering what all the fuss is about.

During World War II, the Japanese military was desperately short of metals. Many statues, including Hachiko's, were melted down. But Hachiko was not forgotten. In 1947, a few years after the war ended, the son of the original sculptor made a new statue of Hachiko. It stands there still.

Every spring, there is a special Hachiko festival at Shibuya Station. It is always held on April 8, one month after Hachiko's death anniversary, when Tokyo's cherry trees are in full bloom. The Shibuya mayor, police chief, and stationmaster are always there. A Shinto priest performs a ceremony, and Hachiko's friends come to admire the beautiful wreaths of flowers that are displayed around his statue.

I thought Hachiko's story was lovely, both sad and wonderful, and I wanted to share it. Kentaro was invented for this story, but I am sure many children who lived near Shibuya Station knew and loved Hachiko.